Incredibly Easy
Cookies

pil

Publications International, Ltd.

Favorite Brand Name Recipes at www.fbnr.com

Microwave Cooking: Microwave ovens vary in wattage. Use the cooking times as guidelines and check for doneness before adding more time.

Preparation/Cooking Times: Preparation times are based on the approximate amount of time required to assemble the recipe before cooking, baking, chilling or serving. These times include preparation steps such as measuring, chopping and mixing. The fact that some preparations and cooking can be done simultaneously is taken into account. Preparation of optional ingredients and serving suggestions is not included.

Table of Contents

Cookie Jar Classics

COCONUT MACAROONS

1 (14-ounce) can **EAGLE BRAND**® Sweetened Condensed
   Milk (NOT evaporated milk)
1 egg white
2 teaspoons vanilla extract
1 to 1½ teaspoons almond extract
2 (7-ounce) packages flaked coconut (5⅓ cups)

1. Preheat oven to 325°F. Line baking sheets with foil; grease and flour foil. Set aside.

2. In large bowl, combine EAGLE BRAND®, egg white, vanilla and almond extract. Stir in coconut. Drop by rounded teaspoonfuls onto prepared baking sheets; with spoon, slightly flatten each mound.

3. Bake 15 to 17 minutes or until golden. Remove from baking sheets; cool on wire racks. Store loosely covered at room temperature. *Makes about 4 dozen cookies*

Prep Time: 10 minutes
Bake Time: 15 to 17 minutes

Coconut Macaroons

OATMEAL TOFFEE BARS

1 cup (2 sticks) butter or margarine, softened
1 cup packed light brown sugar
2 eggs
1 teaspoon vanilla extract
1½ cups all-purpose flour
1 teaspoon baking soda
½ teaspoon ground cinnamon
½ teaspoon salt
1⅓ cups (8-ounce package) HEATH® BITS 'O BRICKLE® Toffee Bits, divided
3 cups quick-cooking or regular rolled oats

1. Heat oven to 350°F. Grease 13×9×2-inch baking pan.

2. Beat butter and brown sugar in large bowl until well blended. Add eggs and vanilla; beat well. Stir together flour, baking soda, cinnamon and salt; gradually add to butter mixture, beating until well blended. Set aside ¼ cup toffee bits. Stir remaining toffee bits and oats into batter (batter will be stiff). Spread batter in prepared pan; sprinkle reserved ¼ cup toffee bits over surface.

3. Bake 25 minutes or until wooden pick inserted in center comes out clean. Cool completely in pan on wire rack. Cut into bars.

Makes about 36 bars

Tip: Bar cookies can be cut into different shapes for variety. To cut into triangles, cut cookie bars into 2- to 3-inch squares, then diagonally cut each square in half. To make diamond shapes, cut parallel lines 2 inches apart across the length of the pan, then cut diagonal lines 2 inches apart.

Oatmeal Toffee Bars

ORIGINAL NESTLÉ® TOLL HOUSE® CHOCOLATE CHIP COOKIES

2¼ cups all-purpose flour
1 teaspoon baking soda
1 teaspoon salt
1 cup (2 sticks) butter or margarine, softened
¾ cup granulated sugar
¾ cup packed brown sugar
1 teaspoon vanilla extract
2 large eggs
2 cups (12-ounce package) NESTLÉ® TOLL HOUSE® Semi-Sweet
    Chocolate Morsels
1 cup chopped nuts

PREHEAT oven to 375°F.

COMBINE flour, baking soda and salt in small bowl. Beat butter, granulated sugar, brown sugar and vanilla extract in large mixer bowl until creamy. Add eggs, one at a time, beating well after each addition. Gradually beat in flour mixture. Stir in morsels and nuts. Drop by rounded tablespoon onto ungreased baking sheets.

BAKE for 9 to 11 minutes or until golden brown. Cool on baking sheets for 2 minutes; remove to wire racks to cool completely.

Makes about 5 dozen cookies

Pan Cookie Variation: **GREASE** 15×10-inch jelly-roll pan. Prepare dough as above. Spread in prepared pan. Bake for 20 to 25 minutes or until golden brown. Cool in pan on wire rack. Makes 4 dozen bars.

Original Nestlé® Toll House® Chocolate Chip Cookies

S'MORE BARS

½ cup (1 stick) butter or margarine
1½ cups graham cracker crumbs
1 (14-ounce) can **EAGLE BRAND®** Sweetened Condensed Milk
   (NOT evaporated milk)
1 cup (6 ounces) milk chocolate or semisweet chocolate chips
1 cup chopped nuts (optional)
1 cup miniature marshmallows

1. Preheat oven to 350°F (325°F for glass dish). In 13×9-inch baking pan, melt butter in oven.

2. Sprinkle graham cracker crumbs evenly over butter; pour EAGLE BRAND® evenly over crumbs. Sprinkle with chocolate chips and nuts (optional); press down gently with fork.

3. Bake 25 minutes. Remove from oven; sprinkle with marshmallows. Return to oven. Bake 2 minutes more. Cool. Chill, if desired. Cut into bars. Store covered at room temperature.

Makes 2 to 3 dozen bars

FIX IT

For easy removal of bar cookies, line the baking pan with foil, leaving at least 3 inches hanging over each end. After baking and cooling, use the foil to lift out the treats and then place them on a cutting board. Remove the foil and cut them into bars.

S'More Bars

TAFFY APPLE COOKIES

½ cup (1 stick) butter, softened
½ cup chunky peanut butter
¾ cup firmly packed light brown sugar
1 egg
1½ cups all-purpose flour
1 teaspoon baking soda
¼ teaspoon baking powder
¼ teaspoon salt
1½ cups butterscotch chips
1 cup chopped dried apples
1 cup caramel apple dip
½ cup chopped peanuts

1. Preheat oven to 350°F. Beat butter, peanut butter and brown sugar in large bowl at medium speed of electric mixer until fluffy. Add egg; beat until well blended.

2. Combine flour, baking soda, baking powder and salt in large bowl. Gradually add to butter mixture, beating until well blended. Stir in butterscotch chips and dried apples.

3. Drop dough by rounded tablespoonfuls 2 inches apart onto ungreased cookie sheets. Bake 8 to 10 minutes or until edges are lightly browned. Cool cookies 2 minutes on cookie sheets. Remove to wire racks; cool completely.

4. Spread about 1 teaspoon caramel apple dip on each cookie. Sprinkle with chopped peanuts.   *Makes about 4 dozen cookies*

BUTTERY ALMOND COOKIES

1¼ cups all-purpose flour
½ teaspoon baking powder
⅛ teaspoon salt
10 tablespoons butter, softened
¾ cup sugar
1 egg
1 teaspoon vanilla
¾ cup slivered almonds, finely chopped
½ cup slivered almonds (optional)

1. Preheat oven to 350°F. Grease cookie sheets. Combine flour, baking powder and salt in small bowl.

2. Beat butter in large bowl with electric mixer at medium speed until smooth. Gradually beat in sugar until blended. Increase speed to high; beat until light and fluffy. Beat in egg and vanilla until fluffy. Stir in flour mixture until blended. Stir in chopped almonds just until blended.

3. Drop rounded teaspoonfuls of dough about 2 inches apart onto prepared cookie sheets. Press several slivered almonds into dough of each cookie, if desired.

4. Bake 12 minutes or until edges are golden brown. Let cookies stand on cookie sheets 5 minutes; transfer to wire racks to cool completely. Store in airtight container.

Makes about 3½ dozen cookies

MAGIC COOKIE BARS

½ cup (1 stick) butter or margarine
1½ cups graham cracker crumbs
1 (14-ounce) can EAGLE BRAND® Sweetened Condensed Milk
   (NOT evaporated milk)
2 cups (12 ounces) semisweet chocolate chips
1⅓ cups flaked coconut
1 cup chopped nuts

1. Preheat oven to 350°F (325°F for glass dish). In 13×9-inch baking pan, melt butter in oven.

2. Sprinkle graham cracker crumbs evenly over butter; pour EAGLE BRAND® evenly over crumbs. Layer evenly with remaining ingredients; press down firmly.

3. Bake 25 minutes or until lightly browned. Cool. Cut into bars. Store loosely covered at room temperature.

Makes 2 to 3 dozen bars

Bake Time: 25 minutes

7-Layer Magic Cookie Bars: Substitute 1 cup (6 ounces) butterscotch-flavored chips for 1 cup semisweet chocolate chips. (Peanut butter-flavored chips or white chocolate chips can be substituted for butterscotch-flavored chips.)

Magic Peanut Cookie Bars: Substitute 2 cups (about ¾ pound) chocolate-covered peanuts for semisweet chocolate chips and chopped nuts.

Magic Rainbow Cookie Bars: Substitute 2 cups plain candy-coated chocolate pieces for semisweet chocolate chips.

Magic Cookie Bars

IRRESISTIBLE PEANUT BUTTER COOKIES

1¼ cups firmly packed light brown sugar
¾ cup JIF® Creamy Peanut Butter
½ CRISCO® Butter Flavor Stick or ½ cup CRISCO® Butter Flavor
    Shortening
3 tablespoons milk
1 tablespoon vanilla
1 egg
1¾ cups PILLSBURY BEST® All-Purpose Flour
¾ teaspoon baking soda
¾ teaspoon salt

1. Preheat oven to 375°F. Place sheets of foil on countertop for cooling cookies.

2. Combine brown sugar, peanut butter, ½ cup shortening, milk and vanilla in large bowl. Beat at medium speed of electric mixer until well blended. Add egg. Beat just until blended.

3. Combine flour, baking soda and salt in medium bowl. Add to creamed mixture at low speed. Mix just until blended.

4. Drop dough by rounded measuring tablespoonfuls 2 inches apart onto ungreased baking sheet. Flatten slightly in crisscross pattern with tines of fork.

5. Bake one baking sheet at a time at 375°F for 7 to 8 minutes, or until set and just beginning to brown. *Do not overbake.* Cool 2 minutes on baking sheet. Remove cookies to foil to cool completely.

Makes about 3 dozen cookies

Irresistible Peanut Butter Cookies

WHITE CHOCOLATE SQUARES

1 (12-ounce) package white chocolate chips, divided
¼ cup (½ stick) butter or margarine
1 (14-ounce) can EAGLE BRAND® Sweetened Condensed Milk
    (NOT evaporated milk)
1 egg
1 teaspoon vanilla extract
2 cups all-purpose flour
½ teaspoon baking powder
1 cup chopped pecans, toasted
    Powdered sugar

1. Preheat oven to 350°F. Grease 13×9-inch baking pan. In large saucepan over low heat, melt 1 cup white chocolate chips and butter. Stir in EAGLE BRAND®, egg and vanilla. Stir in flour and baking powder until blended. Stir in pecans and remaining white chocolate chips. Spoon mixture into prepared pan.

2. Bake 20 to 25 minutes. Cool. Sprinkle with powdered sugar; cut into squares. Store covered at room temperature.

Makes 2 dozen squares

Prep Time: 15 minutes
Bake Time: 20 to 25 minutes

 FIX IT

To toast pecans, spread them in a single layer on a baking sheet and bake in a preheated 350°F oven for 8 to 10 minutes or until very lightly browned. Let them cool slightly before using.

White Chocolate Squares

TOFFEE CHUNK BROWNIE COOKIES

1 cup (2 sticks) butter
4 ounces unsweetened chocolate, coarsely chopped
1½ cups sugar
2 eggs
1 tablespoon vanilla
3 cups all-purpose flour
⅛ teaspoon salt
1½ cups coarsely chopped chocolate-covered toffee bars

1. Preheat oven to 350°F. Melt butter and chocolate in large saucepan over low heat, stirring until smooth. Remove from heat; cool slightly.

2. Stir sugar into chocolate mixture until smooth. Stir in eggs and vanilla until well blended. Stir in flour and salt just until blended. Fold in chopped toffee bars.

3. Drop heaping tablespoonfuls of dough 1½ inches apart onto ungreased cookie sheets.

4. Bake 12 minutes or until just set. Let cookies stand on cookie sheets 5 minutes; transfer to wire racks to cool completely. Store in airtight container.   *Makes 3 dozen cookies*

Toffee Chunk Brownie Cookies

Ginger Shortbread Delights

1 cup (2 sticks) unsalted butter, softened
½ cup powdered sugar
⅓ cup packed light brown sugar
½ teaspoon salt
2 cups minus 2 tablespoons all-purpose flour
4 ounces crystallized ginger
Bittersweet Glaze (recipe follows)

1. Preheat oven to 300°F.

2. Beat butter, sugars and salt in large bowl until creamy. Gradually add flour, beating until well blended.

3. Shape dough by tablespoons into balls. Place 1 inch apart on ungreased cookie sheets; flatten to ½-inch thickness. Cut ginger into ¼-inch-thick slices. Place 1 slice ginger on top of each cookie.

4. Bake 20 minutes or until set and lightly browned. Cool 5 minutes on cookie sheets. Remove to wire racks to cool completely.

5. Prepare Bittersweet Glaze; drizzle over cookies. Let stand about 30 minutes or until glaze is set.   *Makes about 3½ dozen cookies*

Bittersweet Glaze

1 bar (3 to 3.5 ounces) bittersweet chocolate, broken into small
    pieces
2 tablespoons unsalted butter
2 tablespoons whipping cream
1 tablespoon powdered sugar
⅛ teaspoon salt

Melt chocolate and butter in top of double boiler over hot, not boiling, water. Remove from heat. Add cream, powdered sugar and salt; stir until smooth.

Tip: If you are unable to find crystallized ginger, place a pecan or walnut half in the center of each dough ball before baking.

Ginger Shortbread Delights

CANDY BAR BARS

¾ cup (1½ sticks) butter or margarine, softened
¼ cup peanut butter
1 cup firmly packed light brown sugar
1 teaspoon baking soda
2 cups quick-cooking oats
1½ cups all-purpose flour
1 egg
1 (14-ounce) can EAGLE BRAND® Sweetened Condensed Milk
  (NOT evaporated milk)
4 cups chopped candy bars (such as chocolate-covered caramel-
  topped nougat bars with peanuts, chocolate-covered crisp
  wafers, chocolate-covered caramel-topped cookie bars or
  chocolate-covered peanut butter cups)

1. Preheat oven to 350°F. In large bowl, combine butter and peanut butter. Add brown sugar and baking soda; beat well. Stir in oats and flour. Reserve 1¾ cups crumb mixture.

2. Stir egg into remaining crumb mixture; press firmly on bottom of ungreased 15×10×1-inch baking pan. Bake 15 minutes.

3. Pour EAGLE BRAND® evenly over baked crust. Stir together reserved crumb mixture and candy bar pieces; sprinkle evenly over top. Bake 25 minutes or until golden. Cool. Cut into bars. Store covered at room temperature.   *Makes 4 dozen bars*

Prep Time: 20 minutes
Bake Time: 40 minutes

Candy Bar Bars

OATMEAL BUTTERSCOTCH COOKIES

¾ cup (1½ sticks) butter or margarine, softened
¾ cup granulated sugar
¾ cup packed light brown sugar
 2 eggs
 1 teaspoon vanilla extract
1¼ cups all-purpose flour
 1 teaspoon baking soda
½ teaspoon salt
½ teaspoon ground cinnamon
 3 cups quick-cooking or regular rolled oats, uncooked
1¾ cups (11-ounce package) HERSHEY'S Butterscotch Chips

1. Heat oven to 375°F.

2. Beat butter, granulated sugar and brown sugar with electric mixer on medium speed in large bowl until well blended. Add eggs and vanilla; blend thoroughly. Stir together flour, baking soda, salt and cinnamon; gradually add to butter mixture, beating until well blended. Stir in oats and butterscotch chips; mix well. Drop by teaspoons onto ungreased cookie sheet.

3. Bake 8 to 10 minutes or until golden brown. Cool slightly. Remove to wire rack and cool completely.

Makes about 4 dozen cookies

Oatmeal Butterscotch Cookies

NAOMI'S REVEL BARS

1 cup (2 sticks) plus 2 tablespoons butter, softened and divided

2 cups packed brown sugar

2 eggs

2 teaspoons vanilla

2½ cups all-purpose flour

1 teaspoon baking soda

3 cups uncooked old-fashioned or quick oats

1 package (12 ounces) semisweet chocolate chips

1 can (14 ounces) sweetened condensed milk

1. Preheat oven to 325°F. Lightly grease 13×9-inch baking pan.

2. Beat 1 cup butter and brown sugar in large bowl with electric mixer at medium speed until light and fluffy. Add eggs; beat until blended. Stir in vanilla.

3. Combine flour and baking soda in medium bowl. Add flour mixture to butter mixture; beat until well blended. Stir in oats. Spread three fourths of oat mixture evenly in prepared pan.

4. Combine chocolate chips, condensed milk and remaining 2 tablespoons butter in small heavy saucepan. Stir over low heat until chocolate is melted. Pour chocolate mixture evenly over oat mixture in pan. Dot with remaining oat mixture.

5. Bake 20 to 25 minutes or until edges are browned and center feels firm to touch. Cool completely in pan on wire rack. Cut into bars.

Makes about 3 dozen bars

Naomi's Revel Bars

GRANDMA'S OLD-FASHIONED OATMEAL COOKIES

2 cups sugar

1 cup shortening

2 eggs

3½ cups all-purpose flour

3 cups uncooked old-fashioned oats

1 teaspoon baking soda

1 teaspoon salt

1 teaspoon ground cinnamon

1 cup buttermilk

1 cup raisins

1. Preheat oven to 350°F. Lightly grease cookie sheets.

2. Beat sugar and shortening in large bowl with electric mixer at medium speed until creamy. Beat in eggs, one at a time, until mixture is light and fluffy.

3. Combine flour, oats, baking soda, salt and cinnamon in separate bowl. Beat into shortening mixture, ⅓ at a time, alternating with buttermilk until well blended. Stir in raisins.

4. Drop dough by rounded tablespoonfuls onto prepared cookie sheets. Bake 12 to 15 minutes or until lightly browned. Cool slightly on cookie sheets. Remove to wire racks; cool completely. Store at room temperature in airtight containers.

Makes 4 to 5 dozen cookies

Grandma's Old-Fashioned Oatmeal Cookies

CHOCOLATE PISTACHIO COOKIES

2 cups shelled pistachio nuts, finely chopped, divided
1¾ cups all-purpose flour
¼ cup unsweetened cocoa powder
¾ teaspoon baking soda
½ teaspoon salt
¾ cup plus 1 tablespoon I CAN'T BELIEVE IT'S NOT BUTTER!®
    Spread, divided
1 cup granulated sugar
¾ cup firmly packed brown sugar
2 eggs
3 squares (1 ounce each) unsweetened chocolate, melted
½ teaspoon vanilla extract
⅛ teaspoon almond extract
1½ squares (1 ounce each) unsweetened chocolate
2 tablespoons confectioners' sugar

Preheat oven to 375°F. Spray baking sheets with I Can't Believe It's Not Butter!® Spray; set aside. Reserve 3 tablespoons pistachios. In medium bowl, mix flour, cocoa, baking soda and salt; set aside.

In large bowl, with electric mixer, beat ¾ cup I Can't Believe It's Not Butter!® Spread, granulated sugar and brown sugar until light and fluffy, about 5 minutes. Beat in eggs, one at a time, beating 30 seconds after each addition. Beat in melted chocolate and extracts. Beat in flour mixture just until blended. Stir in pistachios.

On prepared baking sheets, drop dough by rounded tablespoonfuls, 1 inch apart. Bake one sheet at a time 8 minutes or until tops are puffed and dry but still soft when touched. *Do not overbake.* On wire rack, cool 5 minutes; remove from sheets and cool completely.

For icing, in microwave-safe bowl, melt 1½ squares chocolate with remaining 1 tablespoon I Can't Believe It's Not Butter! Spread at HIGH (Full Power) 1 minute or until chocolate is melted; stir until smooth. Stir in confectioners' sugar. Spread ¼ teaspoon icing on each cookie; sprinkle with reserved pistachios. Let stand 20 minutes before serving.   *Makes about 3½ dozen cookies*

Chocolate Pistachio Cookies

Outrageous Bars

STREUSEL CARAMEL BARS

2 cups all-purpose flour
¾ cup firmly packed light brown sugar
1 egg, beaten
¾ cup (1½ sticks) cold butter or margarine, divided
¾ cup chopped nuts
24 caramels, unwrapped
1 (14-ounce) can EAGLE BRAND® Sweetened Condensed Milk (NOT evaporated milk)

1. Preheat oven to 350°F. Grease 13×9-inch baking pan. In large bowl, combine flour, brown sugar and egg; cut in ½ cup butter until crumbly. Stir in nuts. Reserve 2 cups crumb mixture. Press remaining crumb mixture firmly on bottom of prepared pan. Bake 15 minutes.

2. Meanwhile, in heavy saucepan over low heat, melt caramels and remaining ¼ cup butter with EAGLE BRAND®. Pour evenly over baked crust. Top with reserved crumb mixture.

3. Bake 20 minutes or until bubbly. Cool. Cut into bars. Store loosely covered at room temperature.

Makes 2 to 3 dozen bars

Prep Time: 25 minutes
Bake Time: 35 minutes

Streusel Caramel Bars

CHOCOLATE DREAM BARS

2¼ cups all-purpose flour, divided
1 cup (2 sticks) butter, softened
¾ cup powdered sugar
⅓ cups unsweetened cocoa powder
2 cups granulated sugar
4 eggs, beaten
4 squares (1 ounce each) unsweetened baking chocolate, melted
Additional powdered sugar for garnish (optional)

1. Preheat oven to 350°F.

2. Combine 2 cups flour, butter, powdered sugar and cocoa in large bowl; beat until well blended and stiff dough forms. Press firmly into ungreased 13×9-inch baking dish. Bake 15 to 20 minutes or just until set. Do not overbake.

3. Meanwhile, combine remaining ¼ cup flour and granulated sugar in medium bowl. Stir in eggs and melted chocolate; beat until blended. Pour over crust.

4. Bake 25 minutes or until toothpick inserted into center comes out clean. Cool completely in pan on wire rack. Sprinkle with powdered sugar, if desired. Cut into bars.   *Makes 3 dozen bars*

Tip: To make a powdered sugar design on these bars, place a stencil, doily or strips of paper over the tops of the bars before dusting them with powdered sugar. Carefully lift off the stencil, doily or paper strips, holding firmly by the edges and pulling straight up.

Chocolate Dream Bars

RAZZ-MA-TAZZ BARS

½ cup (1 stick) butter or margarine
2 cups (12-ounce package) NESTLÉ® TOLL HOUSE® Premier White
    Morsels, *divided*
2 large eggs
½ cup granulated sugar
1 cup all-purpose flour
½ teaspoon salt
½ teaspoon almond extract
½ cup seedless raspberry jam
¼ cup toasted sliced almonds

PREHEAT oven to 325°F. Grease and sugar 9-inch square baking pan.

MELT butter in medium, microwave-safe bowl on HIGH (100%) power for 1 minute; stir. Add *1 cup* morsels; let stand. Do not stir.

BEAT eggs in large mixer bowl until foamy. Add sugar; beat until light lemon colored, about 5 minutes. Stir in morsel-butter mixture. Add flour, salt and almond extract; mix at low speed until combined. Spread ⅔ of batter into prepared pan.

BAKE for 15 to 17 minutes or until light golden brown around edges. Remove from oven to wire rack.

HEAT jam in small, microwave-safe bowl on HIGH (100%) power for 30 seconds; stir. Spread jam over warm crust. Stir *remaining* morsels into *remaining* batter. Drop spoonfuls of batter over jam. Sprinkle with almonds.

BAKE for 25 to 30 minutes or until edges are browned. Cool completely in pan on wire rack. Cut into bars. *Makes 16 bars*

Razz-Ma-Tazz Bars

CAPPUCCINO CRUNCH BARS

1¾ cups all-purpose flour, sifted
1 teaspoon baking soda
1 teaspoon salt
½ teaspoon ground cinnamon
1 cup (2 sticks) butter, softened
1½ cups firmly packed brown sugar
½ cup granulated sugar
2 eggs
2 teaspoons instant coffee granules or espresso powder, dissolved
    in 1 tablespoon hot water and cooled to room temperature
2 teaspoons vanilla
1 teaspoon freshly grated orange peel (optional)
1 cup white chocolate chips
1 cup chocolate-covered toffee bits

1. Preheat oven to 350°F. Grease 13×9-inch baking pan.

2. Combine flour, baking soda, salt and cinnamon in large bowl; set aside.

3. Beat butter and sugars with electric mixer at medium speed until fluffy. Add eggs, one at a time, beating well after each addition. Add coffee mixture, vanilla and orange peel, if desired; beat well. Add flour mixture; beat until well blended. Stir in white chocolate chips and toffee bits.

4. Spread batter evenly in prepared pan. Bake 25 to 35 minutes or until golden brown. Cool completely in pan on wire rack; cut into bars. *Makes about 2½ dozen bars*

PEANUT BUTTER & JELLY STREUSEL BARS

1¼ cups firmly packed light brown sugar
¾ cup JIF® Creamy Peanut Butter
½ CRISCO® Stick or ½ cup CRISCO® shortening plus additional for
    greasing
3 tablespoons milk
1 tablespoon vanilla
1 egg
1¾ cups PILLSBURY BEST® All-Purpose Flour
¾ teaspoon baking soda
¾ teaspoon salt
1 cup SMUCKER'S® Strawberry Jam, stirred
½ cup quick oats, uncooked

1. Heat oven to 350°F. Grease 13×9-inch baking pan. Place cooling rack on countertop.

2. Place brown sugar, peanut butter, ½ cup shortening, milk and vanilla in large bowl. Beat at medium speed of electric mixer until well blended. Add egg; beat just until blended.

3. Combine flour, baking soda and salt. Add to shortening mixture; beat at low speed just until blended.

4. Press ⅔ of dough onto bottom of prepared baking pan. Spread jam over dough to within ¼ inch of edges.

5. Stir oats into remaining dough. Drop dough by spoonfuls onto jam.

6. Bake at 350°F for 20 to 25 minutes or until edges and streusel topping are lightly browned. *Do not overbake.* Cool completely on cooling rack. Cut into 2×1½-inch bars.

Makes about 3 dozen bars

White Chip Lemon Streusel Bars

1 can (14 ounces) sweetened condensed milk (not evaporated milk)
½ cup lemon juice
1 teaspoon freshly grated lemon peel
2 cups (12-ounce package) HERSHEY'S Premier White Chips, divided
⅔ cup butter or margarine, softened
1 cup packed light brown sugar
1½ cups all-purpose flour
1½ cups regular rolled or quick-cooking oats
¾ cup toasted pecan pieces*
1 teaspoon baking powder
½ teaspoon salt
1 egg
½ teaspoon shortening

*To toast pecans: Heat oven to 350°F. Spread pecans in thin layer in shallow baking pan. Bake, stirring occasionally, 7 to 8 minutes or until golden brown; cool.

1. Heat oven to 350°F. Lightly grease 13×9×2-inch baking pan. Combine sweetened condensed milk, lemon juice and lemon peel in medium bowl; set aside. Measure out ¼ cup and ⅓ cup white chips; set aside. Add remaining white chips to lemon mixture.

2. Beat butter and brown sugar with electric mixer on medium speed in large bowl until well blended. Stir together flour, oats, pecans, baking powder and salt; add to butter mixture, blending well. Set aside 1⅔ cups oats mixture. Add egg to remaining oats mixture, blending until crumbly; press onto bottom of prepared pan. Gently spoon lemon mixture on top, spreading evenly. Add reserved ⅓ cup white chips to reserved oats mixture. Sprinkle over lemon layer, pressing down lightly.

3. Bake 20 to 25 minutes or until lightly browned. Cool in pan on wire rack. Place remaining ¼ cup white chips and shortening in small microwave-safe bowl. Microwave at HIGH (100%) 30 seconds or until chips are melted and mixture is smooth when stirred. Drizzle over baked bars. Allow drizzle to set; cut into bars.

Makes 36 bars

White Chip Lemon Streusel Bars

Chocolate Nut Bars

1¾ cups graham cracker crumbs
½ cup (1 stick) butter or margarine, melted
2 cups (12 ounces) semisweet chocolate chips, divided
1 (14-ounce) can EAGLE BRAND® Sweetened Condensed Milk
(NOT evaporated milk)
1 teaspoon vanilla extract
1 cup chopped nuts

1. Preheat oven to 375°F. In medium bowl, combine graham cracker crumbs and butter; press firmly on bottom of ungreased 13×9-inch baking pan. Bake 8 minutes. Reduce oven temperature to 350°F.

2. In small saucepan over low heat, melt 1 cup chocolate chips with EAGLE BRAND® and vanilla. Spread chocolate mixture over baked crust. Top with remaining 1 cup chocolate chips and nuts; press down firmly.

3. Bake 25 to 30 minutes. Cool. Chill, if desired. Cut into bars. Store loosely covered at room temperature.

Makes 2 to 3 dozen bars

Prep Time: 10 minutes
Bake Time: 33 to 38 minutes

 Fix It Fast

Warm nuts are easier to chop than cold or room temperature nuts. Place 1 cup of shelled nuts in a microwavable dish and microwave on HIGH for about 30 seconds or just until warm; chop as desired.

Chocolate Nut Bars

PREMIER CHEESECAKE CRANBERRY BARS

2 cups all-purpose flour

1½ cups quick or old-fashioned oats

¼ cup packed light brown sugar

1 cup (2 sticks) butter or margarine, softened

2 cups (12-ounce package) NESTLÉ® TOLL HOUSE® Premier White
    Morsels

1 package (8 ounces) cream cheese, softened

1 can (14 ounces) NESTLÉ® CARNATION® Sweetened Condensed
    Milk

¼ cup lemon juice

1 teaspoon vanilla extract

1 can (16 ounces) whole-berry cranberry sauce

2 tablespoons cornstarch

PREHEAT oven to 350°F. Grease 13×9-inch baking pan.

COMBINE flour, oats and brown sugar in large bowl. Add butter; mix until crumbly. Stir in morsels. Reserve *2½ cups* morsel mixture for topping. With floured fingers, press *remaining* mixture into prepared pan.

BEAT cream cheese in large mixer bowl until creamy. Add sweetened condensed milk, lemon juice and vanilla extract; mix until smooth. Pour over crust. Combine cranberry sauce and cornstarch in medium bowl. Spoon over cream cheese mixture. Sprinkle *reserved* morsel mixture over cranberry mixture.

BAKE for 35 to 40 minutes or until center is set. Cool completely in pan on wire rack. Cover; refrigerate until serving time (up to 1 day). Cut into bars.   *Makes 2½ dozen bars*

Premier Cheesecake Cranberry Bar

COCOA BOTTOM BANANA PECAN BARS

1 cup sugar
½ cup (1 stick) butter, softened
5 ripe bananas, mashed
1 egg
1 teaspoon vanilla
1½ cups all-purpose flour
1 teaspoon baking powder
1 teaspoon baking soda
½ teaspoon salt
½ cup chopped pecans
¼ cup unsweetened cocoa powder

1. Preheat oven to 350°F. Grease 13×9-inch pan; set aside.

2. Combine sugar and butter in large bowl; beat until creamy. Add bananas, egg and vanilla; beat until well blended. Combine flour, baking powder, baking soda and salt in medium bowl. Add to banana mixture; beat until well blended. Stir in pecans.

3. Divide batter in half. Stir cocoa into one half. Spread cocoa batter in prepared pan. Spread plain batter over cocoa batter; swirl with knife.

4. Bake 30 to 35 minutes or until edges are lightly browned and toothpick inserted into center comes out clean. Cool completely in pan on wire rack. Cut into squares.   *Makes 15 to 18 servings*

Cocoa Bottom Banana Pecan Bars

CHEWY TOFFEE ALMOND BARS

1 cup (2 sticks) butter, softened
½ cup sugar
2 cups all-purpose flour
1⅓ cups (8-ounce package) HEATH® BITS 'O BRICKLE® Almond Toffee
   Bits
¾ cup light corn syrup
1 cup sliced almonds, divided
¾ cup MOUNDS® Sweetened Coconut Flakes, divided

1. Heat oven to 350°F. Grease sides of 13×9×2-inch baking pan.

2. Beat butter and sugar with electric mixer on medium speed in large bowl until fluffy. Gradually add flour, beating until well blended. Press dough evenly into prepared pan. Bake 15 to 20 minutes or until edges are lightly browned.

3. Meanwhile, combine toffee bits and corn syrup in medium saucepan. Cook over medium heat, stirring constantly, until toffee is melted (about 10 to 12 minutes). Stir in ½ cup almonds and ½ cup coconut. Spread toffee mixture to within ¼ inch of edges of crust. Sprinkle remaining ½ cup almonds and remaining ¼ cup coconut over top.

4. Bake an additional 15 minutes or until bubbly. Cool completely in pan on wire rack. Cut into bars.   *Makes 36 bars*

Chewy Toffee Almond Bars

CHOCOLATE ORANGE CHEESECAKE BARS

Crust
- 1 cup all-purpose flour
- ½ cup packed light brown sugar
- ¼ teaspoon ground cinnamon (optional)
- ⅓ cup shortening
- ½ cup chopped pecans

Chocolate Orange Filling
- 1 package (8 ounces) cream cheese, softened
- ⅔ cup granulated sugar
- ⅓ cup HERSHEY'S Cocoa
- ¼ cup milk
- 1 egg
- 1 teaspoon vanilla extract
- ¼ teaspoon freshly grated orange peel
- Pecan halves (optional)

1. Heat oven to 350°F.

2. For crust, stir together flour, brown sugar and cinnamon, if desired, in large bowl. Cut shortening into flour mixture with pastry blender or two knives until mixture resembles coarse crumbs. Stir in chopped pecans. Reserve ¾ cup flour mixture. Press remaining mixture firmly onto bottom of ungreased 9-inch square baking pan. Bake 10 minutes or until lightly browned.

3. For chocolate orange filling, beat cream cheese and sugar with electric mixer on medium speed in medium bowl until fluffy. Add cocoa, milk, egg, vanilla and orange peel; beat until smooth.

4. Spread filling over warm crust. Sprinkle with reserved flour mixture. Press pecan halves lightly onto top, if desired. Return to oven. Bake 25 to 30 minutes or until lightly browned. Cool; cut into bars. Cover; refrigerate leftover bars.   *Makes 24 bars*

Chocolate Orange Cheesecake Bars

CHUNKY PECAN PIE BARS

Crust
  1½ cups all-purpose flour
  ½ cup (1 stick) butter or margarine, softened
  ¼ cup packed brown sugar

Filling
  3 large eggs
  ¾ cup corn syrup
  ¾ cup granulated sugar
  2 tablespoons butter or margarine, melted
  1 teaspoon vanilla extract
  1¾ cups (11.5-ounce package) NESTLÉ® TOLL HOUSE® Semi-Sweet
    Chocolate Chunks
  1½ cups coarsely chopped pecans

PREHEAT oven to 350°F. Grease 13×9-inch baking pan.

For Crust
BEAT flour, butter and brown sugar in small mixer bowl until crumbly. Press into prepared baking pan.

BAKE for 12 to 15 minutes or until lightly browned.

For Filling
BEAT eggs, corn syrup, granulated sugar, butter and vanilla extract in medium bowl with wire whisk. Stir in chunks and nuts. Pour evenly over baked crust.

BAKE for 25 to 30 minutes or until set. Cool completely in pan on wire rack. Cut into bars.   *Makes 2 to 3 dozen bars*

Chunky Pecan Pie Bars

POLKA DOT COCONUT MACAROON BARS

3¾ cups MOUNDS® Sweetened Coconut Flakes
¾ cup sugar
¼ cup all-purpose flour
¼ teaspoon salt
3 egg whites
1 whole egg, slightly beaten
1 teaspoon almond extract
1 cup HERSHEY'S MINI KISSES® Brand Milk Chocolates

1. Heat oven to 350°F. Lightly grease 9-inch square baking pan.

2. Stir together coconut, sugar, flour and salt in large bowl. Add egg whites, whole egg and almond extract; stir until well blended. Stir in chocolate pieces. Spread mixture in prepared pan, covering all chocolate pieces with coconut mixture.

3. Bake 35 minutes or until lightly browned. Cool completely in pan on wire rack. Cover with foil; allow to stand at room temperature about 8 hours or overnight. Cut into bars.

Makes about 24 bars

Prep Time: 15 minutes
Bake Time: 35 minutes
Cool Time: 9 hours

Variation: Omit chocolate pieces in batter. Immediately after removing pan from oven, place desired number of chocolate pieces on top, pressing down lightly. Cool completely. Cut into bars.

Polka Dot Coconut Macaroon Bars

STRAWBERRY OAT BARS

1 cup (2 sticks) butter, softened
1 cup packed light brown sugar
2 cups uncooked quick oats
1 cup all-purpose flour
2 teaspoons baking soda
½ teaspoon ground cinnamon
¼ teaspoon salt
1 can (21 ounces) strawberry pie filling
¾ teaspoon almond extract

1. Preheat oven to 375°F. Beat butter in large bowl with electric mixer at medium speed until smooth. Add brown sugar; beat until well blended.

2. Combine oats, flour, baking soda, cinnamon and salt in large bowl; mix well. Add flour mixture to butter mixture, beating at low speed until well blended and crumbly.

3. Spread two thirds of crumb mixture on bottom of ungreased 13×9-inch baking pan, pressing to form firm layer. Bake 15 minutes; let cool 5 minutes on wire rack.

4. Meanwhile, place strawberry filling in food processor or blender. Cover and process until smooth. Stir in almond extract.

5. Pour strawberry mixture over partially baked crust. Sprinkle remaining crumb mixture evenly over strawberry layer.

6. Return pan to oven; bake 20 to 25 minutes or until topping is golden brown and filling is slightly bubbly. Cool completely on wire rack. Cut into bars.   *Makes about 4 dozen bars*

Strawberry Oat Bars

Marbled Cheesecake Bars

2 cups finely crushed creme-filled chocolate sandwich cookies
(about 24 cookies)
3 tablespoons butter or margarine, melted
3 (8-ounce) packages cream cheese, softened
1 (14-ounce) can EAGLE BRAND® Sweetened Condensed Milk
(NOT evaporated milk)
3 eggs
2 teaspoons vanilla extract
2 (1-ounce) squares unsweetened chocolate, melted

1. Preheat oven to 300°F. Line 13×9-inch baking pan with foil; set aside. In medium bowl, combine cookie crumbs and butter; press firmly on bottom of prepared pan.

2. In large bowl, beat cream cheese until fluffy. Gradually beat in EAGLE BRAND® until smooth. Add eggs and vanilla; mix well. Pour half the batter evenly over prepared crust.

3. Stir melted chocolate into remaining batter; spoon over vanilla batter. With table knife or metal spatula, gently swirl through batter to marble.

4. Bake 45 to 50 minutes or until set. Cool. Chill. Cut into bars. Store covered in refrigerator.   *Makes 2 to 3 dozen bars*

Prep Time: 20 minutes
Bake Time: 45 to 50 minutes

Tip: For even marbling, do not oversoften or overbeat the cream cheese.

Marbled Cheesecake Bars

Chocolate Chip Shortbread

½ cup (1 stick) butter, softened
½ cup sugar
 1 teaspoon vanilla
 1 cup all-purpose flour
¼ teaspoon salt
½ cup mini semisweet chocolate chips

1. Preheat oven to 375°F.

2. Beat butter and sugar in large bowl with electric mixer at medium speed until light and fluffy. Beat in vanilla. Add flour and salt; beat at low speed. Stir in chocolate chips.

3. Divide dough in half. Press each half into ungreased 8-inch round cake pan.

4. Bake 12 minutes or until edges are golden brown. Score shortbread with sharp knife, taking care not to cut completely through shortbread. Make 8 triangles per pan.

5. Let pans stand on wire racks 10 minutes. Invert shortbread onto wire racks; cool completely. Break into triangles.

Makes 16 cookies

Fix It *Fast*

Softening butter in the microwave is quick and easy! Place 1 stick of butter on a microwavable plate and microwave on LOW (30%) for about 30 seconds or just until softened.

Chocolate Chip Shortbread

Irresistible Brownies

REESE'S® PEANUT BUTTER AND MILK CHOCOLATE CHIP BROWNIES

¾ cup **HERSHEY'S Cocoa**
½ **teaspoon baking soda**
⅔ **cup butter or margarine, melted and divided**
½ **cup boiling water**
2 **cups sugar**
2 **eggs**
1⅓ **cups all-purpose flour**
1 **teaspoon vanilla extract**
¼ **teaspoon salt**
1¾ **cups (11-ounce package) REESE'S® Peanut Butter and Milk Chocolate Chips**

1. Heat oven to 350°F. Grease 13×9×2-inch baking pan.

2. Stir together cocoa and baking soda in large bowl; stir in ⅓ cup melted butter. Add boiling water; stir until mixture thickens. Stir in sugar, eggs and remaining ⅓ cup melted butter; stir until smooth. Add flour, vanilla and salt; blend thoroughly. Stir in chips. Pour into prepared pan.

3. Bake 35 to 40 minutes or until brownies begin to pull away from sides of pan. Cool completely in pan on wire rack. Cut into squares.   *Makes about 36 brownies*

Reese's® Peanut Butter and Milk Chocolate Chip Brownies

DULCE DE LECHE BLONDIES

2 cups all-purpose flour
1 teaspoon baking soda
1 teaspoon salt
1 cup (2 sticks) unsalted butter, softened
1 cup firmly packed brown sugar
2 eggs
1½ teaspoons vanilla
1 (14-ounce) package caramels
½ cup evaporated milk

1. Preheat oven to 350°F. Grease 13×9-inch baking pan. Sift together flour, baking soda and salt in medium bowl; set aside.

2. Beat butter and brown sugar in large bowl until creamy. Add eggs and vanilla; beat until smooth. Gradually stir in flour mixture. Spread half to two thirds of batter in prepared pan. Bake 7 to 8 minutes. Let cool 5 minutes on wire rack.

3. Meanwhile, melt caramels with evaporated milk in nonstick saucepan over very low heat; reserve 2 tablespoons. Pour remaining caramel mixture over baked bottom layer. Drop dollops of remaining batter over caramel layer; swirl slightly with knife.

4. Bake 25 minutes or until golden brown. Cool completely in pan on wire rack. Cut into squares. Reheat reserved caramel, if necessary; drizzle over blondies.   *Makes about 3 dozen blondies*

Dulce de Leche Blondies

TRIPLE CHOCOLATE BROWNIES

½ cup (1 stick) butter
3 squares (1 ounce each) unsweetened chocolate, coarsely
    chopped
2 squares (1 ounce each) semisweet chocolate, coarsely chopped
1 cup all-purpose flour
½ teaspoon salt
¼ teaspoon baking powder
1½ cups sugar
3 eggs
1 teaspoon vanilla
¼ cup sour cream
½ cup milk chocolate chips
    Powdered sugar (optional)

1. Preheat oven to 350°F. Lightly grease 13×9-inch baking pan.

2. Place butter, unsweetened chocolate and semisweet chocolate in medium microwavable bowl. Microwave on HIGH 2 minutes or until butter is melted; stir until chocolate is completely melted and mixture is smooth. Cool to room temperature.

3. Combine flour, salt and baking powder in small bowl; set aside. Beat sugar, eggs and vanilla in large bowl with electric mixer at medium speed until slightly thickened. Beat in chocolate mixture until well blended. Add flour mixture; beat at low speed until blended. Add sour cream; beat at low speed until blended. Stir in milk chocolate chips. Spread mixture evenly in prepared pan.

4. Bake 20 to 25 minutes or until toothpick inserted into center comes out almost clean. (Do not overbake.) Cool brownies completely in pan on wire rack. Cut into 2-inch squares. Sprinkle with powdered sugar, if desired.   *Makes 2 dozen brownies*

Triple Chocolate Brownies

LAYERS OF LOVE CHOCOLATE BROWNIES

¾ cup all-purpose flour
¾ cup NESTLÉ® TOLL HOUSE® Baking Cocoa
¼ teaspoon salt
½ cup (1 stick) butter, cut in pieces
½ cup granulated sugar
½ cup packed brown sugar
 3 large eggs, *divided*
 2 teaspoons vanilla extract
 1 cup chopped pecans
¾ cup NESTLÉ® TOLL HOUSE® Premier White Morsels
½ cup caramel ice cream topping
¾ cup NESTLÉ® TOLL HOUSE® Semi-Sweet Chocolate Morsels

PREHEAT oven to 350°F. Grease 8-inch square baking pan.

COMBINE flour, cocoa and salt in small bowl. Beat butter, granulated sugar and brown sugar in large mixer bowl until creamy. Add *2 eggs*, one at a time, beating well after each addition. Add vanilla extract; mix well. Gradually beat in flour mixture. Reserve *¾ cup* batter. Spread *remaining* batter into prepared baking pan. Sprinkle pecans and white morsels over batter. Drizzle caramel topping over top. Beat *remaining* egg and *reserved* batter in same large bowl until light in color. Stir in semi-sweet morsels. Spread evenly over caramel topping.

BAKE for 30 to 35 minutes or until center is set. Cool completely in pan on wire rack. Cut into squares. *Makes 16 brownies*

Layers of Love Chocolate Brownies

BLACK RUSSIAN BROWNIES

4 squares (1 ounce each) unsweetened chocolate
1 cup butter
¾ teaspoon ground black pepper
4 eggs, lightly beaten
1½ cups granulated sugar
1½ teaspoons vanilla
⅓ cup KAHLÚA® Liqueur
2 tablespoons vodka
1⅓ cups all-purpose flour
½ teaspoon salt
¼ teaspoon baking powder
1 cup chopped walnuts or toasted sliced almonds
Powdered sugar (optional)

Preheat oven to 350°F. Line bottom of 13×9-inch baking pan with waxed paper. Melt chocolate and butter with pepper in small saucepan over low heat, stirring until smooth. Remove from heat; cool.

Combine eggs, granulated sugar and vanilla in large bowl; beat well. Stir in cooled chocolate mixture, Kahlúa and vodka. Combine flour, salt and baking powder; add to chocolate mixture and stir until blended. Add walnuts. Spread evenly in prepared pan.

Bake just until wooden toothpick inserted into center comes out clean, about 25 minutes. *Do not overbake.* Cool in pan on wire rack. Cut into bars. Sprinkle with powdered sugar.

Makes about 2½ dozen brownies

"BLONDIE" BROWNIES

½ **CRISCO®** Butter Flavor Stick or ½ cup **CRISCO®** Butter Flavor
  shortening plus additional for greasing
1 tablespoon milk
1 cup firmly packed brown sugar
1 egg
1 cup **PILLSBURY BEST®** All-Purpose Flour
½ teaspoon baking powder
⅛ teaspoon salt
½ cup chopped walnuts
1 teaspoon vanilla

1. Heat oven to 350°F. Grease 8×8×2-inch pan with shortening. Place cooling rack on countertop.

2. Combine ½ cup shortening and milk in large microwave-safe bowl. Microwave at 50% (MEDIUM). Stir after 1 minute. Repeat until melted (or melt on rangetop in large saucepan on low heat). Stir in sugar. Stir in egg quickly. Combine flour, baking powder and salt. Stir into sugar mixture. Stir in nuts and vanilla. Spread in prepared pan.

3. Bake at 350°F for 27 to 30 minutes, or until toothpick inserted in center comes out clean. *Do not overbake.* Cool in pan on cooling rack. Cut into 2×2-inch squares. *Makes 16 squares*

DOUBLE-DECKER CONFETTI BROWNIES

¾ cup (1½ sticks) butter or margarine, softened
1 cup granulated sugar
1 cup firmly packed light brown sugar
3 large eggs
1 teaspoon vanilla extract
2½ cups all-purpose flour, divided
2½ teaspoons baking powder
½ teaspoon salt
⅓ cup unsweetened cocoa powder
1 tablespoon butter or margarine, melted
1 cup "M&M's"® Semi-Sweet Chocolate Mini Baking Bits, divided

Preheat oven to 350°F. Lightly grease 13×9×2-inch baking pan; set aside. In large bowl cream ¾ cup butter and sugars until light and fluffy; beat in eggs and vanilla. In medium bowl combine 2¼ cups flour, baking powder and salt; blend into creamed mixture. Divide batter in half. Blend together cocoa powder and melted butter; stir into one half of the dough. Spread cocoa dough evenly into prepared baking pan. Stir remaining ¼ cup flour and ½ cup "M&M's"® Semi-Sweet Chocolate Mini Baking Bits into remaining dough; spread evenly over cocoa dough in pan. Sprinkle with remaining ½ cup "M&M's"® Semi-Sweet Chocolate Mini Baking Bits. Bake 25 to 30 minutes or until edges start to pull away from sides of pan. Cool completely. Cut into bars. Store in tightly covered container.   *Makes 24 brownies*

Double-Decker Confetti Brownies

CHUNKY CARAMEL NUT BROWNIES

4 squares (1 ounce each) unsweetened chocolate
¾ cup (1½ sticks) butter
2 cups sugar
4 eggs
1 cup all-purpose flour
1 package (14 ounces) caramels
¼ cup heavy cream
2 cups pecan halves or coarsely chopped pecans, divided
1 package (12 ounces) chocolate chunks or chips

1. Preheat oven to 350°F. Grease 13×9-inch baking pan; set aside.

2. Place chocolate and butter in large microwavable bowl. Microwave on HIGH 1½ to 2 minutes or until chocolate is melted and mixture is smooth when stirred. Stir in sugar until well blended. Beat in eggs, one at a time. Stir in flour until well blended. Spread half of batter in prepared pan. Bake 20 minutes.

3. Meanwhile, combine caramels and cream in medium microwavable bowl. Microwave on HIGH 1½ to 2 minutes or until caramels begin to melt; stir until mixture is smooth. Stir in 1 cup pecan halves.

4. Spread caramel mixture over partially baked brownie base. Sprinkle with half of chocolate chunks. Pour remaining brownie batter over top; sprinkle with remaining 1 cup pecan halves and chocolate chunks. Bake 25 to 30 minutes or until set. Cool completely in pan on wire rack. Cut into squares.

Makes 2 dozen brownies

Chunky Caramel Nut Brownies

CHOCOLATE MARBLED BLONDIES

½ cup (1 stick) butter or margarine, softened
½ cup firmly packed light brown sugar
1 large egg
2 teaspoons vanilla extract
1½ cups all-purpose flour
1¼ teaspoons baking soda
1 cup "M&M's"® Chocolate Mini Baking Bits, divided
4 ounces cream cheese, softened
2 tablespoons granulated sugar
1 large egg yolk
¼ cup unsweetened cocoa powder

Preheat oven to 350°F. Lightly grease 9×9×2-inch baking pan; set aside. In large bowl cream butter and brown sugar until light and fluffy; beat in egg and vanilla. In medium bowl combine flour and baking soda; blend into creamed mixture. Stir in ⅔ cup "M&M's"® Chocolate Mini Baking Bits; set aside. Dough will be stiff. In separate bowl beat together cream cheese, granulated sugar and egg yolk until smooth; stir in cocoa powder until well blended. Place chocolate-cheese mixture in six equal portions evenly onto bottom of prepared pan. Place reserved dough around cheese mixture and swirl slightly with tines of fork. Pat down evenly on top. Sprinkle with remaining ⅓ cup "M&M's"® Chocolate Mini Baking Bits. Bake 25 to 30 minutes or until toothpick inserted in center comes out with moist crumbs. Cool completely. Cut into bars. Store in refrigerator in tightly covered container.   *Makes 16 bars*

Chocolate Marbled Blondies

CHOCOLATEY ROCKY ROAD BROWNIES

Brownies
- 1 cup (2 sticks) butter
- 4 squares (1 ounce each) unsweetened chocolate
- 1½ cups granulated sugar
- 1 cup all-purpose flour
- 3 eggs
- 1½ teaspoons vanilla
- ½ cup chopped salted peanuts

Frosting
- ¼ cup (½ stick) butter
- 1 package (3 ounces) cream cheese
- 1 square (1 ounce) unsweetened chocolate
- ¼ cup milk
- 2¾ cups powdered sugar
- 1 teaspoon vanilla
- 2 cups miniature marshmallows
- 1 cup salted peanuts

1. For brownies, preheat oven to 350°F. Grease 13×9-inch baking pan. Set aside.

2. Combine butter and chocolate in 3-quart saucepan. Cook over medium heat, stirring constantly, until melted, 5 to 7 minutes. Add granulated sugar, flour, eggs and vanilla; mix well. Stir in peanuts. Spread in prepared pan. Bake 20 to 25 minutes or until brownie starts to pull away from sides of pan. Cool completely in pan on wire rack.

3. For frosting, combine butter, cream cheese, chocolate and milk in 2-quart saucepan. Cook over medium heat, stirring occasionally, until melted, 6 to 8 minutes. Remove from heat; add powdered sugar and vanilla; beat until smooth. Stir in marshmallows and peanuts. Immediately spread over cooled brownies. Cool completely; cut into bars. Store leftovers covered in refrigerator.

Makes about 4 dozen brownies

Chocolatey Rocky Road Brownies

WHITE CHOCOLATE & ALMOND BROWNIES

½ **cup (1 stick) unsalted butter**
8 **squares (1 ounce each) white chocolate**
3 **eggs**
¾ **cup sugar**
1 **cup all-purpose flour**
1 **teaspoon vanilla**
¼ **teaspoon salt**
½ **cup slivered almonds**

1. Preheat oven to 325°F. Lightly grease 9-inch square baking pan. Melt butter in medium saucepan over low heat. (Do not let butter turn brown.) Remove from heat; add white chocolate. Swirl butter to cover chocolate. (Do not stir.)

2. Beat eggs 30 seconds in large bowl. Gradually beat in sugar; continue beating 2 to 3 minutes or until mixture turns pale yellow. Beat in white chocolate mixture, flour, vanilla and salt just until smooth. Pour batter evenly into prepared pan; sprinkle with almonds.

3. Bake 35 to 40 minutes or until center is completely set. If necessary, cover pan loosely with foil during last 10 minutes of baking to prevent overbrowning. Cool completely in pan on wire rack. Cut into squares. *Makes about 16 brownies*

FUDGY CHEESECAKE SWIRL BROWNIES

¾ cup (1½ sticks) butter or margarine

2 bars (2 ounces *each*) NESTLÉ® TOLL HOUSE® Unsweetened
    Chocolate Baking Bars, broken into pieces

2¼ cups granulated sugar, *divided*

4 large eggs, *divided*

1¾ cups all-purpose flour

1 package (8 ounces) cream cheese, softened

1 teaspoon vanilla extract

PREHEAT oven to 350°F. Grease 13×9-inch baking pan.

MELT butter and baking bars in medium, *heavy-duty* saucepan over low heat, stirring until smooth. Cool to room temperature. Stir in *1¾ cups* sugar. Beat in *3 eggs;* stir in flour. Spread into prepared baking pan.

BEAT cream cheese and *remaining ½ cup* sugar in small mixer bowl. Beat in *remaining* egg and vanilla extract. Pour over chocolate mixture; deeply swirl batters with knife.

BAKE for 30 to 35 minutes or until wooden pick inserted near center comes out slightly sticky. Cool completely in pan on wire rack.   *Makes 2 dozen brownies*

BLAST-OFF BROWNIES

4 (1-ounce) squares unsweetened chocolate
¾ cup (1½ sticks) butter or margarine
2 cups sugar
1 cup flour
3 eggs
1 tablespoon TABASCO® brand Pepper Sauce
½ cup semisweet chocolate chips
½ cup walnuts, chopped

Preheat oven to 350°F. Grease 9×9-inch baking pan. Melt chocolate and butter in small saucepan over medium-low heat, stirring frequently. Combine sugar, flour, eggs, TABASCO® Sauce and melted chocolate mixture in large bowl until well blended. Stir in chocolate chips and walnuts. Spoon mixture into prepared pan. Bake 35 to 40 minutes or until toothpick inserted in center comes out clean. Cool in pan on wire rack.   *Makes 16 brownies*

FIX IT Fast

To measure flour accurately, spoon it into a measuring cup to overflowing and then with the straight edge of a knife or metal spatula, sweep across the top of the cup to level the flour. Do not dip the cup into the flour, because this will compact the flour and result in an inaccurate measure.

Blast-Off Brownies

RASPBERRY FUDGE BROWNIES

½ cup (1 stick) butter

3 squares (1 ounce each) bittersweet chocolate*

1 cup sugar

2 eggs

1 teaspoon vanilla

¾ cup all-purpose flour

¼ teaspoon baking powder

   Dash salt

½ cup sliced or slivered almonds

½ cup raspberry preserves

1 cup (6 ounces) milk chocolate chips

*One square unsweetened chocolate plus two squares semisweet chocolate can be substituted.

1. Preheat oven to 350°F. Lightly grease and flour 8-inch square baking pan.

2. Melt butter and bittersweet chocolate in small, heavy saucepan over low heat. Remove from heat; cool. Beat sugar, eggs and vanilla in large bowl until light. Beat in chocolate mixture. Stir in flour, baking powder and salt until just blended. Spread three fourths of batter in prepared pan; sprinkle with almonds.

3. Bake 10 minutes. Remove from oven; spread preserves over almonds. Carefully spoon remaining batter over preserves, smoothing top. Bake 25 to 30 minutes or just until top feels firm.

4. Immediately sprinkle chocolate chips over top. Let stand 1 to 2 minutes or until chips melt; spread evenly over brownies. Cool completely in pan on wire rack. Let stand until chocolate is set. Cut into 2-inch squares. *Makes 16 brownies*

Raspberry Fudge Brownies

BUTTERSCOTCH BLONDIES

¾ cup (1½ sticks) butter or margarine, softened
¾ cup packed light brown sugar
½ cup granulated sugar
2 eggs
2 cups all-purpose flour
1 teaspoon baking soda
½ teaspoon salt
1¾ cups (11-ounce package) HERSHEY'S Butterscotch Chips
1 cup chopped nuts (optional)

1. Preheat oven to 350°F. Grease 13×9×2-inch baking pan.

2. Beat butter, brown sugar and granulated sugar in large bowl until creamy. Add eggs; beat well. Stir together flour, baking soda and salt; gradually add to butter mixture, blending well. Stir in butterscotch chips and nuts, if desired. Spread into prepared pan.

3. Bake 30 to 35 minutes or until top is golden brown and center is set. Cool completely in pan on wire rack. Cut into bars.

Makes about 36 bars

FIX IT Fast

To soften hard, lumpy brown sugar, place it in a microwavable bowl and cover with plastic wrap. Microwave on HIGH for 30 to 45 seconds; stir and repeat if necessary. Watch the brown sugar carefully to make sure it doesn't melt. If it does start to melt, remove it from the microwave and let it stand about 1 minute, then stir.

Butterscotch Blondies

ORANGE CAPPUCCINO BROWNIES

¾ cup (1½ sticks) butter
2 squares (1 ounce each) semisweet chocolate, coarsely chopped
2 squares (1 ounce each) unsweetened chocolate, coarsely chopped
1¾ cups sugar
1 tablespoon instant espresso powder or instant coffee granules
3 eggs
¼ cup orange-flavored liqueur
2 teaspoons freshly grated orange peel
1 cup all-purpose flour
1 package (12 ounces) semisweet chocolate chips
2 tablespoons shortening

1. Preheat oven to 350°F. Grease 13×9-inch baking pan.

2. Melt butter and chopped chocolate squares in large heavy saucepan over low heat, stirring constantly. Stir in sugar and espresso powder. Remove from heat; cool slightly. Beat in eggs, one at a time. Stir in liqueur and orange peel. Add flour; beat just until blended. Spread batter evenly in prepared pan. Bake 25 to 30 minutes or until center is just set. Remove pan to wire rack.

3. Combine chocolate chips and shortening in small microwavable bowl. Microwave on HIGH 1 minute; stir. Microwave for 30-second intervals, stirring after each interval, until chocolate is melted and mixture is smooth. Immediately spread melted chocolate mixture over warm brownies. Cool completely in pan on wire rack. Cut into bars.   *Makes about 2 dozen brownies*

Orange Cappuccino Brownies

MARBLED PEANUT BUTTER BROWNIES

½ cup (1 stick) butter, softened
¼ cup peanut butter
1 cup packed light brown sugar
½ cup granulated sugar
3 eggs
1 teaspoon vanilla
2 cups all-purpose flour
2 teaspoons baking powder
⅛ teaspoon salt
1 cup chocolate syrup
½ cup coarsely chopped salted mixed nuts

1. Preheat oven to 350°F. Lightly grease 13×9-inch baking pan.

2. Beat butter and peanut butter in large bowl until blended; stir in sugars. Beat in eggs, one at a time, until well blended. Blend in vanilla. Combine flour, baking powder and salt in small bowl. Stir into butter mixture.

3. Spread half of batter evenly in prepared pan. Spread syrup over top. Spoon remaining batter over syrup. Swirl with knife or spatula to create marbled effect. Sprinkle with chopped nuts. Bake 35 to 40 minutes or until lightly browned. Cool completely in pan on wire rack. Cut into 2-inch squares.

Makes about 2 dozen brownies

Marbled Peanut Butter Brownies

Just for Kids

SPACE DUST BARS

1 package (12 ounces) white chocolate chips
⅓ cup butter
2 cups graham cracker crumbs
1 cup chopped pecans
2 cans (12 ounces each) apricot dessert and pastry filling
1 cup sweetened flaked coconut
Additional sweetened flaked coconut or powdered sugar (optional)

1. Preheat oven to 350°F. Grease 13×9-inch baking pan. Combine white chocolate chips and butter in medium saucepan; cook and stir over low heat until melted and smooth. Remove from heat; stir in graham cracker crumbs and pecans. Let cool 5 minutes.

2. Press half of crumb mixture onto bottom of prepared pan. Bake 10 minutes or until golden brown. Remove from oven; spread apricot filling evenly over crust. Combine coconut with remaining crumb mixture; sprinkle evenly over top of apricot filling. Bake 20 to 25 minutes or until light golden brown. Cool completely in pan on wire rack. Sprinkle with additional coconut or powdered sugar, if desired. Cut into bars.

Makes 1½ dozen bars

Space Dust Bars

PEPPERMINT PIGS

1 package (18 ounces) refrigerated sugar cookie dough
½ cup all-purpose flour
¾ teaspoon peppermint extract
Red food coloring
Prepared white icing and mini candy-coated chocolate pieces

1. Preheat oven to 350°F. Lightly grease cookie sheets. Let dough stand at room temperature about 15 minutes.

2. Combine dough, flour, peppermint extract and food coloring in large bowl; beat at medium speed of electric mixer until well blended and evenly colored. Divide dough into 20 equal pieces. For each pig, shape 1 dough piece into 1 (1-inch) ball, 1 (½-inch) ball and 2 (¼-inch) balls. Flatten 1-inch ball to ¼-inch-thick round; place on prepared cookie sheet. Flatten ½-inch ball to ¼-inch-thick oval; place on top of dough round for snout. Shape 2 (¼-inch) balls into triangles; fold point over and place at top of round for ears. Make indentations in snout for nostrils with wooden skewer.

3. Bake 9 to 11 minutes or until set. Remove to wire racks; cool completely. Use white icing and candy-coated chocolate pieces to make eyes as shown in photo.   *Makes 20 cookies*

Peppermint Pigs

S'MORE BARS

1 package (18 ounces) refrigerated chocolate chip cookie dough
¼ cup graham cracker crumbs
3 cups mini marshmallows
½ cup semisweet or milk chocolate chips
2 teaspoons shortening

1. Preheat oven to 350°F. Grease 13×9-inch baking pan. Press dough into prepared pan. Sprinkle evenly with graham cracker crumbs.

2. Bake 10 to 12 minutes or until edges are golden brown. Sprinkle with marshmallows. Bake 2 to 3 minutes or until marshmallows are puffed. Cool completely in pan on wire rack.

3. Combine chocolate chips and shortening in small resealable food storage bag; seal. Microwave on HIGH 1 minute; knead bag lightly. Microwave on HIGH for additional 30-second intervals until chips and shortening are completely melted and smooth, kneading bag after each 30-second interval. Cut off small corner of bag. Drizzle over bars. Refrigerate 5 to 10 minutes or until chocolate is set. Cut into bars.   *Makes 3 dozen bars*

S'More Bars

Banana Split Sundae Cookies

1 cup (2 sticks) margarine or butter, softened
1 cup firmly packed brown sugar
1½ cups mashed ripe bananas (about 4 medium)
2 eggs
2 teaspoons vanilla
2½ cups QUAKER® Oats (quick or old fashioned, uncooked)
2 cups all-purpose flour
1 teaspoon baking soda
¼ teaspoon salt (optional)
1 cup (6 ounces) semisweet chocolate pieces
Ice cream or frozen yogurt
Ice cream topping, any flavor

Heat oven to 350°F. Beat together margarine and sugar until creamy. Add bananas, eggs and vanilla; beat well. Add combined oats, flour, baking soda and salt; mix well. Stir in chocolate pieces; mix well. Drop by ¼ cupfuls onto ungreased cookie sheets about 3 inches apart. Spread dough to 3½-inch diameter. Bake 14 to 16 minutes or until edges are light golden brown. Cool 1 minute on cookie sheets; remove to wire racks. Cool completely. To serve, top each cookie with scoop of ice cream and ice cream topping.

Makes about 2 dozen cookies

CHEWY ROCKY ROAD BARS

1½ cups finely crushed unsalted pretzels

¾ cup (1½ sticks) butter or margarine, melted

1 can (14 ounces) sweetened condensed milk (not evaporated milk)

2 cups miniature marshmallows

1 cup HERSHEY'S Butterscotch Chips

1 cup HERSHEY'S Semi-Sweet Chocolate Chips

1 cup MOUNDS® Sweetened Coconut Flakes

¾ cup chopped nuts

1. Heat oven to 350°F.

2. Combine crushed pretzels and butter in small bowl; lightly press mixture onto bottom of ungreased 13×9×2-inch baking pan. Pour sweetened condensed milk evenly over crumb mixture. Top with marshmallows, butterscotch chips, chocolate chips, coconut and nuts. Press toppings firmly into sweetened condensed milk.

3. Bake 25 to 30 minutes or until lightly browned. Cool completely in pan on wire rack. Cut into bars.   *Makes about 36 bars*

Variations: 2 cups (12-ounce package) HERSHEY'S Semi-Sweet Chocolate Chips OR 1¾ cups (11-ounce package) HERSHEY'S Butterscotch Chips can be used instead of 1 cup of each flavor.

Bamboozlers

1 cup all-purpose flour
¾ cup packed light brown sugar
¼ cup unsweetened cocoa powder
1 egg
2 egg whites
5 tablespoons margarine, melted
¼ cup fat-free (skim) milk
¼ cup honey
1 teaspoon vanilla
2 tablespoons semisweet chocolate chips
2 tablespoons coarsely chopped walnuts
Powdered sugar (optional)

1. Preheat oven to 350°F. Grease and flour 8-inch square baking pan; set aside.

2. Combine flour, brown sugar and cocoa in medium bowl. Blend together egg, egg whites, margarine, milk, honey and vanilla in medium bowl. Add to flour mixture; mix well. Pour into prepared pan; sprinkle with chocolate chips and walnuts.

3. Bake brownies about 30 minutes or until they spring back when lightly touched in center. Cool completely in pan on wire rack. Sprinkle with powdered sugar just before serving, if desired. Cut into bars. *Makes 1 dozen brownies*

Peanutters: Substitute peanut butter chips for chocolate chips and peanuts for walnuts.

Butterscotch Babies: Substitute butterscotch chips for chocolate chips and pecans for walnuts.

Bamboozlers

COOKIE NUGGETS

35 rich round crackers
1 package (18 ounces) refrigerated chocolate chip cookie dough with peanut butter filling (20 count)
Honey and strawberry or raspberry jam

1. Preheat oven to 350°F. Grease cookie sheets. Let dough stand at room temperature about 15 minutes.

2. Meanwhile, place crackers in resealable food storage bag; seal bag. Crush crackers with rolling pin until fine crumbs form. Reserve ½ cup crumbs.

3. Combine dough and remaining crumbs in large bowl; beat at medium speed of electric mixer until well blended. Shape 2 rounded teaspoonfuls of dough into oval; flatten slightly. Roll in reserved crumbs; place on prepared cookie sheets. Pinch in sides of oval to make cookie resemble chicken nugget. Repeat with remaining dough and crumbs.

4. Bake 8 to 10 minutes or until set. Cool on cookie sheets 10 minutes. Remove to wire racks; cool completely.

5. Serve cookies with honey and jam for dipping.

Makes about 2½ dozen cookies

Tip: If dough becomes too soft to shape, refrigerate 15 minutes.

Cookie Nuggets

BROWNIE TURTLE COOKIES

2 squares (1 ounce each) unsweetened baking chocolate
⅓ cup solid vegetable shortening
1 cup granulated sugar
2 large eggs
½ teaspoon vanilla extract
1¼ cups all-purpose flour
½ teaspoon baking powder
½ teaspoon salt
1 cup "M&M's"® Milk Chocolate Mini Baking Bits, divided
1 cup pecan halves
⅓ cup caramel ice cream topping
⅓ cup shredded coconut
⅓ cup finely chopped pecans

Preheat oven to 350°F. Lightly grease cookie sheets; set aside. Heat chocolate and shortening in 2-quart saucepan over low heat, stirring constantly until melted; remove from heat. Mix in sugar, eggs and vanilla. Blend in flour, baking powder and salt. Stir in ⅔ cup "M&M's"® Milk Chocolate Mini Baking Bits. For each cookie, arrange 3 pecan halves, with ends almost touching at center, on prepared cookie sheets. Drop dough by rounded teaspoonfuls onto center of each group of pecans; mound the dough slightly. Bake 8 to 10 minutes or just until set. *Do not overbake.* Cool completely on wire racks. In small bowl combine ice cream topping, coconut and chopped nuts; top each cookie with about 1½ teaspoons mixture. Press remaining ⅓ cup "M&M's"® Milk Chocolate Mini Baking Bits into topping.   *Makes about 2½ dozen cookies*

Brownie Turtle Cookies

"EVERYTHING BUT THE KITCHEN SINK" BAR COOKIES

1 package (18 ounces) refrigerated chocolate chip cookie dough
1 jar (7 ounces) marshmallow creme
½ cup creamy peanut butter
1½ cups toasted corn cereal
½ cup miniature candy-coated chocolate pieces

1. Preheat oven to 350°F. Grease 13×9-inch baking pan. Press dough into prepared pan. Bake 13 minutes.

2. Remove from oven. Drop teaspoonfuls of marshmallow creme and peanut butter over hot cookie base. Bake 1 minute.

3. Carefully spread marshmallow creme and peanut butter over cookie base. Sprinkle with cereal and chocolate pieces.

4. Bake 7 minutes. Cool completely in pan on wire rack. Cut into 2-inch bars.

Makes 3 dozen bars

FIX IT *Fast*

Before measuring the peanut butter, spray the measuring cup with nonstick cooking spray or lightly grease it with vegetable oil. That way the peanut butter will slide right out and not stick to the cup.

"Everything but the Kitchen Sink" Bar Cookies

CHILD'S CHOICE

2⅓ cups PILLSBURY BEST® All-Purpose Flour
1 CRISCO® Butter Flavor Stick or 1 cup CRISCO® Butter Flavor
    shortening plus additional for greasing
1 teaspoon baking soda
½ teaspoon baking powder
1 cup granulated sugar
1 cup firmly packed brown sugar
2 eggs
1 teaspoon maple flavor
2 cups oats (quick or old-fashioned, uncooked)
¾ cup semisweet chocolate chips
¾ cup miniature marshmallows
¾ cup peanut butter chips

1. Heat oven to 350°F. Grease baking sheet with shortening. Place sheets of foil on countertop for cooling cookies.

2. Combine flour, 1 cup shortening, baking soda and baking powder in large bowl. Beat at low speed of electric mixer until blended. Increase speed to medium; mix thoroughly. Beat in granulated sugar, brown sugar, eggs and maple flavor. Add oats. Stir in chocolate chips, marshmallows and peanut butter chips with spoon until well blended.

3. Shape dough into 1½-inch balls. Flatten slightly. Place 2 inches apart on prepared baking sheet.

4. Bake at 350°F for 9 to 10 minutes or until light golden brown. *Do not overbake.* Cool 2 minutes on baking sheet. Remove cookies to foil to cool completely.   *Makes about 3½ dozen cookies*

Child's Choice

ANIMAL PAWPRINTS

1 package (18 ounces) refrigerated sugar cookie dough
¼ cup unsweetened cocoa powder
Regular-sized and mini peanut butter chips

1. Preheat oven to 350°F. Grease cookie sheets. Let dough stand at room temperature about 15 minutes.

2. Combine dough and cocoa in large bowl; beat at medium speed of electric mixer until well blended. For each cookie, shape dough into 1 (1-inch) ball and 4 (¼-inch) balls. Place large ball on prepared cookie sheet; place smaller balls on one side of large ball as shown in photo.

3. Bake 12 to 14 minutes or until cookies are set and no longer shiny. Remove from oven; immediately place regular-sized peanut butter chip on first "toe" and place mini peanut butter chips on remaining "toes" of each cookie. Transfer cookies to wire racks to cool completely. *Makes 1½ dozen cookies*

 FIX IT *Fast*

When a recipe calls for greasing the cookie sheets, use shortening or a vegetable cooking spray for the best results. Lining the cookie sheets with parchment paper is an alternative to greasing. It eliminates cleanup, bakes the cookies more evenly and allows them to cool right on the paper instead of on wire racks.

Animal Pawprints

Color-Bright Ice Cream Sandwiches

¾ cup (1½ sticks) butter or margarine, softened
¾ cup creamy peanut butter
1¼ cups firmly packed light brown sugar
 1 large egg
 1 teaspoon vanilla extract
1½ cups all-purpose flour
 1 teaspoon baking soda
 ¼ teaspoon salt
1¾ cups "M&M's"® Chocolate Mini Baking Bits, divided
 2 quarts vanilla or chocolate ice cream, slightly softened

Preheat oven to 350°F. In large bowl cream butter, peanut butter and sugar until light and fluffy; beat in egg and vanilla. In medium bowl combine flour, baking soda and salt; blend into creamed mixture. Stir in 1⅓ cups "M&M's"® Chocolate Mini Baking Bits. Shape dough into 1¼-inch balls. Place about 2 inches apart on ungreased cookie sheets. Gently flatten to about ½-inch thickness with fingertips. Place 7 or 8 of the remaining "M&M's"® Chocolate Mini Baking Bits on each cookie; press in lightly. Bake 10 to 12 minutes or until edges are light brown. *Do not overbake.* Cool about 1 minute on cookie sheets; cool completely on wire racks. Assemble cookies in pairs with about ⅓ cup ice cream; press cookies together lightly. Wrap each sandwich in plastic wrap; freeze until firm.   *Makes about 24 ice cream sandwiches*

Color-Bright Ice Cream Sandwiches

Sweet Nutty O's

1 package (18 ounces) refrigerated sugar cookie dough
1 cup finely chopped honey-roasted peanuts, divided
¼ cup all-purpose flour
2 tablespoons honey
1 egg white, lightly beaten

1. Preheat oven to 350°F. Lightly grease cookie sheets. Let dough stand at room temperature about 15 minutes.

2. Combine dough, ¾ cup peanuts, flour and honey in large bowl; beat at medium speed of electric mixer until well blended.

3. For each cookie, shape about 1 tablespoon dough into 4-inch-long rope. Press ends together to make ring; place on prepared cookie sheets. Brush with egg white; sprinkle with remaining ¼ cup peanuts.

4. Bake 9 to 11 minutes or until golden brown. Cool on cookie sheets 1 minute. Remove to wire racks; cool completely.

Makes 3 dozen cookies

 Fix It Fast

For even baking and browning of cookies, bake them in the center of the oven. If the heat distribution in your oven is uneven, turn the cookie sheet halfway through the baking time. Most cookies bake quickly and should be watched carefully to avoid overbaking.

Sweet Nutty O's

CRITTERS-IN-HOLES

48 round milk chocolate-covered caramel candies
48 pieces candy corn
    Miniature candy-coated chocolate pieces
  1 container (16 ounces) frosting, any flavor
  1 package (18 ounces) refrigerated peanut butter cookie dough

1. Preheat oven to 350°F. Grease 24 (1¾-inch) mini muffin pan cups.

2. Cut slit into side of 1 caramel candy using sharp knife. Carefully insert 1 piece candy corn into slit. Repeat with remaining caramel candies and candy corn.

3. Attach miniature chocolate pieces to caramel candies to resemble "eyes", using frosting as glue. Decorate as desired.

4. Cut dough into 12 (1-inch) slices. Cut each slice into 4 equal pieces. Using half the pieces, place one dough piece into each prepared muffin cup.

5. Bake 9 minutes. Remove from oven and immediately press 1 decorated caramel candy into center of each cookie. Remove to wire racks; cool completely. Repeat with remaining dough pieces and candies.   *Makes 4 dozen cookies*

Critters-in-Holes

COOKIE PIZZA

1 package (18 ounces) refrigerated sugar or peanut butter cookie
  dough
All-purpose flour (optional)
6 ounces (1 cup) semisweet chocolate chips
1 tablespoon plus 2 teaspoons shortening, divided
  Gummy fruit, chocolate-covered peanuts, assorted roasted nuts,
    raisins, jelly beans and other assorted candies for toppings
¼ cup white chocolate chips

1. Preheat oven to 350°F. Generously grease 12-inch pizza pan. Let dough stand at room temperature about 15 minutes.

2. Press dough onto prepared pan, leaving about ¾ inch between edge of dough and pan. Sprinkle dough with flour to minimize sticking, if necessary.

3. Bake 14 to 23 minutes or until golden brown and set in center. Cool completely in pan on wire rack. Run metal spatula between cookie and pan after 10 to 15 minutes to loosen.

4. Combine semisweet chocolate chips and 1 tablespoon shortening in microwavable bowl. Microwave on HIGH 1 minute; stir. Repeat process at 10- to 20-second intervals until melted and smooth. Spread melted chocolate mixture over crust to within 1 inch of edge. Decorate with desired toppings.

5. Combine white chocolate chips and remaining 2 teaspoons shortening in another microwavable bowl. Microwave on MEDIUM-HIGH (70%) 1 minute; stir. Repeat process at 10- to 20-second intervals until melted and smooth. Drizzle melted white chocolate over toppings to resemble melted mozzarella cheese.

Makes 10 to 12 pizza slices

Cookie Pizza

MUD CUPS

1 package (18 ounces) refrigerated sugar cookie dough
¼ cup unsweetened cocoa powder
3 containers (4 ounces each) prepared chocolate pudding
1¼ cups chocolate sandwich cookie crumbs (about 15 cookies)
Gummy worms

1. Preheat oven to 350°F. Grease 18 (2½- or 2¾-inch) muffin pan cups. Let dough stand at room temperature about 15 minutes.

2. Combine dough and cocoa in large bowl; beat at medium speed of electric mixer until well blended. Shape dough into 18 balls; press onto bottoms and up sides of prepared muffin cups.

3. Bake 12 to 14 minutes or until set. Remove from oven; gently press down center of each cookie with back of teaspoon. Cool in pan 10 minutes. Remove cups from pan; cool completely on wire racks.

4. Fill each cup with 1 to 2 tablespoons pudding; sprinkle with cookie crumbs. Garnish with gummy worms.

Makes 1½ dozen cookie cups

Tip: Chocolate cookie crumbs can be purchased in the baking section of your supermarket.

Mud Cups

Almost
Homemade

CHOCOLATE GINGERSNAPS

¾ cup sugar
1 package (18¼ ounces) chocolate cake mix *without* pudding in the mix
1 tablespoon ground ginger
2 eggs
⅓ cup vegetable oil

1. Preheat oven to 350°F. Spray cookie sheets with nonstick cooking spray. Place sugar in shallow bowl.

2. Combine cake mix and ginger in large bowl. Add eggs and oil; stir until well blended.

3. Shape dough by tablespoonfuls into 1-inch balls; roll in sugar to coat. Place 2 inches apart on prepared cookie sheets.

4. Bake about 10 minutes; transfer to wire racks to cool completely.   *Makes about 3 dozen cookies*

Chocolate Gingersnaps

PUMPKIN CHOCOLATE CHIP SANDWICHES

1 cup solid-pack pumpkin
1 package (18 ounces) refrigerated chocolate chip cookie dough
¾ cup all-purpose flour
½ teaspoon pumpkin pie spice*
½ cup prepared cream cheese frosting

*Substitute ¼ teaspoon ground cinnamon, ⅛ teaspoon ground ginger and pinch each ground allspice and ground nutmeg for ½ teaspoon pumpkin pie spice.

1. Line colander with paper towel. Place pumpkin in prepared colander; drain about 20 minutes to remove excess moisture.

2. Meanwhile, preheat oven to 350°F. Grease cookie sheets. Let dough stand at room temperature about 15 minutes.

3. Combine dough, pumpkin, flour and pumpkin pie spice in large bowl; beat at medium speed of electric mixer until well blended.

4. Drop dough by teaspoonfuls onto prepared cookie sheets. Bake 9 to 11 minutes. Cool on cookie sheets 3 minutes; remove to wire racks to cool completely.

5. Place about 1 teaspoon frosting on flat side of one cookie; top with second cookie. Repeat with remaining cookies and frosting.

Makes about 2 dozen sandwich cookies

Pumpkin Chocolate Chip Sandwiches

CHOCOLATE PEANUT FUDGE BARS

1 package (18 ounces) refrigerated chocolate chip cookie dough
    with peanut butter filling (20 count)
1 package (12 ounces) semisweet chocolate chips
1 cup heavy cream
3 egg yolks, beaten
½ cup all-purpose flour
¼ cup uncooked old-fashioned oats
¼ cup packed brown sugar
3 tablespoons butter
½ cup coarsely chopped salted peanuts

1. Preheat oven to 350°F. Grease 13×9-inch baking pan. Let dough stand at room temperature about 15 minutes.

2. Press dough evenly into pan. Bake 10 minutes. Remove from oven.

3. Combine chocolate chips and cream in small saucepan over low heat. Cook and stir 3 to 4 minutes or until chocolate is melted and mixture is smooth. Remove from heat; stir in egg yolks. Spread chocolate mixture over dough.

4. Combine flour, oats and brown sugar in medium bowl. Cut in butter with pastry blender or two knives until mixture is crumbly. Stir in chopped peanuts. Sprinkle over chocolate layer. Bake 25 to 30 minutes or until just firm. Cool completely in pan on wire rack. Cut into bars.   *Makes 2 dozen bars*

Chocolate Peanut Fudge Bars

ROCKY ROAD SQUARES

1 package (19.5 to 21 ounces) fudge brownie mix
Vegetable oil, per package directions
Large egg(s), per package directions
NESTLÉ® CARNATION® Evaporated Milk
1 cup (6 ounces) NESTLÉ® TOLL HOUSE® Semi-Sweet Chocolate
  Morsels
2 cups miniature marshmallows
1 cup coarsely chopped walnuts

PREHEAT oven according to brownie mix package directions.
Grease 13×9-inch baking pan.

PREPARE brownie mix according to package directions, using
vegetable oil and egg(s) and substituting evaporated milk for water.
Spread into prepared baking pan.

BAKE according to package directions; do not overbake. Remove
from oven. Immediately sprinkle with morsels. Let stand 5 minutes
or until morsels are shiny. Spread evenly. Top with marshmallows
and walnuts.

BAKE for 3 to 5 minutes or just until marshmallows begin to melt.
Cool in pan on wire rack for 20 to 30 minutes. Cut into squares.
Serve warm. *Makes 24 brownies*

FRUIT AND COOKIE PIZZA

1 package (18 ounces) refrigerated chocolate chip cookie dough
1 can (20 ounces) DOLE® Pineapple Slices
1 package (8 ounces) light cream cheese
⅓ cup sugar
1 teaspoon vanilla extract
1 DOLE® Banana, peeled, sliced
½ cup DOLE® Mandarin Oranges, drained
½ cup sliced DOLE® Strawberries
2 to 4 tablespoons bottled chocolate sauce

• Press small pieces of cookie dough onto greased 12-inch pizza pan. Bake at 350°F, 10 to 12 minutes or until browned and puffed. Cool completely in pan on wire rack.

• Drain pineapple slices, reserving 2 tablespoons juice.

• Beat cream cheese, sugar, reserved juice and vanilla in bowl until smooth. Spread over cooled cookie.

• Arrange pineapple slices over cream cheese. Arrange banana slices, oranges and strawberries in pattern over pineapple slices. Drizzle chocolate sauce over fruit. Cut into wedges to serve.

Makes 10 servings

Prep Time: 15 minutes
Bake Time: 12 minutes

BLONDIE BISCOTTI WITH ALMONDS

1 cup slivered almonds
1 package (about 18 ounces) white cake mix
⅔ cup all-purpose flour
2 eggs
3 tablespoons melted butter, cooled slightly
1 teaspoon vanilla
3 tablespoons freshly grated lemon peel

1. Preheat oven to 350°F. Line cookie sheet with parchment paper; set aside.

2. Place medium skillet over medium heat until hot. Add almonds and cook 1½ to 2 minutes or just until fragrant, stirring constantly. *Do not brown.* Set aside.

3. Beat cake mix, flour, eggs, butter and vanilla in large bowl 1 to 2 minutes at low speed of electric mixer or until well blended. Stir in almonds and lemon peel. Knead dough 7 to 8 times or until ingredients are well blended.

4. Divide dough in half. Shape each half into 12×2×½-inch log; place logs 3 inches apart on prepared cookie sheet.

5. Bake 25 minutes or until toothpick inserted into centers of logs comes out clean. Cool on cookie sheet on wire rack 25 minutes.

6. Remove biscotti logs to cutting board, peeling off parchment paper. Using serrated knife, cut each log diagonally into ½-inch slices. Place slices, cut sides down, on cookie sheet; bake 10 minutes or until bottoms of slices are golden brown.

7. Remove biscotti to wire racks; cool completely. Store in airtight container. *Makes about 3 dozen biscotti*

Blondie Biscotti with Almonds

CHOCOLATE MALT DELIGHTS

1 package (18 ounces) refrigerated chocolate chip cookie dough
⅓ cup plus 3 tablespoons malted milk powder, original or chocolate flavor, divided
1¼ cups prepared chocolate frosting
1 cup coarsely chopped malted milk balls

1. Preheat oven to 350°F. Grease cookie sheets. Let dough stand at room temperature about 15 minutes.

2. Combine dough and ⅓ cup malted milk powder in large bowl; beat at medium speed of electric mixer until well blended. Drop rounded tablespoonfuls of dough onto prepared cookie sheets.

3. Bake 10 to 12 minutes or until lightly browned at edges. Cool on cookie sheets 5 minutes; remove to wire racks to cool completely.

4. Combine frosting and remaining 3 tablespoons malted milk powder. Top each cookie with rounded tablespoonful of frosting; garnish with malted milk balls.   *Makes about 1½ dozen cookies*

FIX IT
Fast

If you're baking several batches of cookies, speed things up by placing the cookies onto sheets of foil or parchment paper ahead of time. That way they'll be ready to slide right onto the cookie sheet and into the oven. Make sure to let the cookie sheet cool before you bake another batch on the same one or the dough may melt and spread, changing the shape and texture of the cookies.

Chocolate Malt Delights

LEMON CHEESE BARS

1 package (18¼ ounces) white or yellow cake mix with pudding in the mix
2 eggs
⅓ cup vegetable oil
1 package (8 ounces) cream cheese
⅓ cup sugar
1 teaspoon lemon juice

1. Preheat oven to 350°F.

2. Combine cake mix, 1 egg and oil in large bowl; stir until crumbly. Reserve 1 cup crumb mixture. Press remaining crumb mixture into ungreased 13×9-inch baking pan. Bake 15 minutes or until light golden brown.

3. Combine remaining egg, cream cheese, sugar and lemon juice in medium bowl; beat until smooth and well blended. Spread over baked layer. Sprinkle with reserved crumb mixture. Bake 15 minutes or until cream cheese layer is just set. Cool in pan on wire rack. Cut into bars. *Makes 1½ dozen bars*

Lemon Cheese Bars

Peanut Butter Marbled Brownies

4 ounces cream cheese, softened
½ cup peanut butter
2 tablespoons sugar
1 egg
1 package (20 to 22 ounces) brownie mix, plus ingredients to
prepare mix
¾ cup lightly salted cocktail peanuts

1. Preheat oven to 350°F. Lightly grease 13×9-inch baking pan; set aside.

2. Beat cream cheese, peanut butter, sugar and egg in large bowl with electric mixer at medium speed until blended.

3. Prepare brownie mix according to package directions. Spread brownie batter evenly in prepared pan. Spoon peanut butter mixture in dollops over batter. Swirl peanut butter mixture into batter with tip of knife. Sprinkle peanuts on top; lightly press into batter.

4. Bake 30 to 35 minutes or until toothpick inserted into center comes out almost clean. Do not overbake. Cool brownies completely in pan on wire rack. Cut into squares.   *Makes 2 dozen brownies*

Peanut Butter Marbled Brownies

MAPLE OATMEAL RAISIN DROPS

1 package (18 ounces) refrigerated sugar cookie dough
1 cup uncooked quick oats
1 cup raisins
¼ cup maple syrup
Maple Glaze (recipe follows)

1. Preheat oven to 350°F. Lightly grease cookie sheets. Let dough stand at room temperature about 15 minutes.

2. Combine dough, oats, raisins and maple syrup in large bowl; beat at medium speed of electric mixer until well blended. Drop by rounded teaspoonfuls 2 inches apart onto prepared cookie sheets.

3. Bake 9 to 11 minutes or until edges are lightly browned and center is set. Cool on cookie sheets 1 minute. Remove to wire racks; cool completely.

4. Prepare Maple Glaze; drizzle over cooled cookies. Let stand until set.

Makes 3 dozen cookies

Maple Glaze: Combine 1 cup powdered sugar and 1 tablespoon maple syrup in small bowl; whisk until blended. Add additional maple syrup by teaspoonfuls until glaze is of drizzling consistency.

Maple Oatmeal Raisin Drops

COCONUT CRATERS

1 package (18 ounces) refrigerated chocolate chip cookie dough
¼ cup packed brown sugar
2 tablespoons milk
1 tablespoon butter, melted
1 cup flaked coconut
½ cup chocolate-covered toffee baking bits

1. Preheat oven to 350°F. Line 36 (1¾-inch) mini muffin pan cups with paper baking cups.

2. Shape dough into 36 balls; press onto bottoms and up sides of muffin cups. Bake 9 to 11 minutes or until golden brown.

3. Meanwhile, combine brown sugar, milk and butter in medium bowl. Stir in coconut and toffee bits. Gently press down center of each cookie with back of teaspoon. Spoon 1 rounded teaspoon toffee mixture into each cup. Bake 2 to 4 minutes or until golden. Cool in pan 10 minutes. Remove to wire rack; cool completely.

Makes 3 dozen cookies

Coconut Craters

CHERRY SPICE BARS

1 (10-ounce) jar maraschino cherries
1 (18¼-ounce) package spice cake mix
¼ cup butter or margarine, melted
¼ cup firmly packed brown sugar
¼ cup water
2 eggs

Glaze

1 cup confectioners' sugar
1 tablespoon lemon juice
1 to 2 teaspoons milk

Drain maraschino cherries; discard juice or save for another use. Cut cherries in half. Combine dry cake mix, melted butter, brown sugar, water and eggs in a large mixing bowl; mix with a spoon or electric mixer until well blended and smooth. Stir in maraschino cherries. Spread batter into a greased 13×9×2-inch baking pan.

Bake in a preheated 375°F oven 20 to 25 minutes, or until top springs back when lightly touched. Let cool in pan on wire rack.

For the glaze, combine confectioners' sugar and lemon juice; add enough milk to make a thick glaze. Drizzle glaze over bars. Allow glaze to set. Cut into bars. Store up to one week in an airtight container with sheets of waxed paper between each layer of bars.

Makes 2 dozen bars

Favorite recipe from **Cherry Marketing Institute**

CREAMY CAPPUCCINO BROWNIES

1 package (21 to 24 ounces) brownie mix, plus ingredients to
    prepare mix
1 tablespoon coffee crystals *or* 1 teaspoon espresso powder
2 tablespoons warm water
1 cup (8 ounces) Wisconsin Mascarpone cheese
3 tablespoons granulated sugar
1 egg
    Powdered sugar

Grease bottom of 13×9-inch baking pan. Prepare brownie mix
according to package directions. Pour half of batter into prepared
pan. In medium bowl, dissolve coffee crystals in warm water; add
Mascarpone, granulated sugar and egg. Blend until smooth. Drop
by spoonfuls over brownie batter; top with remaining brownie
batter. With knife, swirl cheese mixture through brownies creating
marbled effect. Bake at 375°F 30 to 35 minutes or until toothpick
inserted in center comes out clean. Sprinkle with powdered sugar.

Makes 2 dozen brownies

Favorite recipe from Wisconsin Milk Marketing Board

FIX IT
Fast

*It may sound strange, but cookies,
brownies and bars make great gifts!
Place them in a paper-lined tin or on
a decorative plate; cover with plastic
wrap and tie with a colorful ribbon.
For a special touch, include the recipe.*

FUDGE-FILLED BARS

1 (12-ounce) package semisweet chocolate chips
2 tablespoons butter or margarine
1 (14-ounce) can EAGLE BRAND® Sweetened Condensed Milk
(NOT evaporated milk)
2 teaspoons vanilla extract
2 (18-ounce) packages refrigerated cookie dough (oatmeal-
chocolate chip, chocolate chip or sugar cookie dough)

1. Preheat oven to 350°F. In heavy saucepan over medium heat, melt chocolate chips and butter with EAGLE BRAND®, stirring often. Remove from heat; stir in vanilla. Cool 15 minutes.

2. Using floured hands, press 1½ packages of cookie dough into ungreased 15×10×1-inch baking pan. Pour cooled chocolate mixture evenly over dough. Crumble remaining dough over chocolate mixture.

3. Bake 25 to 30 minutes. Cool. Cut into bars. Store covered at room temperature.   *Makes 4 dozen bars*

Prep Time: 20 minutes
Bake Time: 25 to 30 minutes

Helpful Hint: If you want to trim the fat in any EAGLE BRAND® recipe, just use EAGLE BRAND® Fat Free or Low Fat Sweetened Condensed Milk instead of the original EAGLE BRAND®.

Fudge-Filled Bars

JAMMY STREUSEL BARS

1 package (18 ounces) refrigerated sugar cookie dough
½ cup strawberry, raspberry or blackberry jam
½ cup all-purpose flour
½ cup packed light brown sugar
¼ cup butter
1 cup sliced almonds or chopped walnuts

1. Preheat oven to 350°F. Grease 13×9-inch baking pan. Let dough stand at room temperature about 15 minutes.

2. Press dough evenly into prepared pan. Spread jam over dough; set aside.

3. Combine flour and brown sugar in medium bowl; cut in butter with pastry blender or two knives until mixture is crumbly. Sprinkle flour mixture over jam layer. Sprinkle with nuts.

4. Bake 25 minutes or until top and edges are lightly browned. Cool completely in pan on wire rack.   *Makes 2½ dozen bars*

Jammy Streusel Bars

CHEESECAKE-TOPPED BROWNIES

1 (19.5- or 19.8-ounce family-size) package fudge brownie mix,
    plus ingredients to prepare mix
1 (8-ounce) package cream cheese, softened
2 tablespoons butter or margarine, softened
1 tablespoon cornstarch
1 (14-ounce) can EAGLE BRAND® Sweetened Condensed Milk
    (NOT evaporated milk)
1 egg
2 teaspoons vanilla extract
    Ready-to-spread chocolate frosting (optional)
    Orange peel (optional)

1. Preheat oven to 350°F. Prepare brownie mix as package directs. Spread into well-greased 13×9-inch baking pan.

2. In large bowl, beat cream cheese, butter and cornstarch until fluffy.

3. Gradually beat in EAGLE BRAND®. Add egg and vanilla; beat until smooth. Pour cheesecake mixture evenly over brownie batter.

4. Bake 40 to 45 minutes or until top is lightly browned. Cool. Spread with frosting or sprinkle with orange peel (optional). Cut into bars. Store leftovers covered in refrigerator.

Makes 3 to 3½ dozen brownies

Prep Time: 20 minutes
Bake Time: 40 to 45 minutes

Cheesecake-Topped Brownies

MOON ROCKS

1 package (18 ounces) refrigerated sugar cookie dough
1 cup uncooked quick oats
¾ cup butterscotch chips
¾ cup yogurt-covered raisins

1. Preheat oven to 350°F. Lightly grease cookie sheets. Let dough stand at room temperature about 15 minutes.

2. Combine dough, oats, butterscotch chips and raisins in large bowl; beat at medium speed of electric mixer until well blended. Drop dough by rounded teaspoonfuls 2 inches apart onto prepared cookie sheets.

3. Bake 9 to 11 minutes or until set. Cool on cookie sheets 1 minute. Remove to wire racks; cool completely.

Makes 3 dozen cookies

FIX IT *Fast*

Cookies that are uniform in size and shape will finish baking at the same time. To easily shape drop cookies into a uniform size, use an ice cream scoop with a release bar. The bar usually has a number on it indicating the number of scoops that can be made from one quart of ice cream. The handiest size for cookies is a #40, #50 or #80 scoop.

Moon Rocks

ACKNOWLEDGMENTS

The publisher would like to thank the companies and organizations listed below for the use of their recipes and photographs in this publication.

Cherry Marketing Institute

Crisco is a registered trademark of The J.M. Smucker Company

Dole Food Company, Inc.

EAGLE BRAND®

The Hershey Company

Jif® trademark of The J.M. Smucker Company

Kahlúa® Liqueur

© Mars, Incorporated 2006

McIlhenny Company (TABASCO® brand Pepper Sauce)

Nestlé USA

The Quaker® Oatmeal Kitchens

Unilever Foods North America

Wisconsin Milk Marketing Board

INDEX

Index

Index

Index

METRIC CONVERSION CHART

VOLUME MEASUREMENTS (dry)

$1/8$ teaspoon = 0.5 mL
$1/4$ teaspoon = 1 mL
$1/2$ teaspoon = 2 mL
$3/4$ teaspoon = 4 mL
1 teaspoon = 5 mL
1 tablespoon = 15 mL
2 tablespoons = 30 mL
$1/4$ cup = 60 mL
$1/3$ cup = 75 mL
$1/2$ cup = 125 mL
$2/3$ cup = 150 mL
$3/4$ cup = 175 mL
1 cup = 250 mL
2 cups = 1 pint = 500 mL
3 cups = 750 mL
4 cups = 1 quart = 1 L

VOLUME MEASUREMENTS (fluid)

1 fluid ounce (2 tablespoons) = 30 mL
4 fluid ounces ($1/2$ cup) = 125 mL
8 fluid ounces (1 cup) = 250 mL
12 fluid ounces ($1 1/2$ cups) = 375 mL
16 fluid ounces (2 cups) = 500 mL

WEIGHTS (mass)

$1/2$ ounce = 15 g
1 ounce = 30 g
3 ounces = 90 g
4 ounces = 120 g
8 ounces = 225 g
10 ounces = 285 g
12 ounces = 360 g
16 ounces = 1 pound = 450 g

DIMENSIONS

$1/16$ inch = 2 mm
$1/8$ inch = 3 mm
$1/4$ inch = 6 mm
$1/2$ inch = 1.5 cm
$3/4$ inch = 2 cm
1 inch = 2.5 cm

OVEN TEMPERATURES

250°F = 120°C
275°F = 140°C
300°F = 150°C
325°F = 160°C
350°F = 180°C
375°F = 190°C
400°F = 200°C
425°F = 220°C
450°F = 230°C

BAKING PAN SIZES

Utensil	Size in Inches/Quarts	Metric Volume	Size in Centimeters
Baking or	$8 \times 8 \times 2$	2 L	$20 \times 20 \times 5$
Cake Pan	$9 \times 9 \times 2$	2.5 L	$23 \times 23 \times 5$
(square or	$12 \times 8 \times 2$	3 L	$30 \times 20 \times 5$
rectangular)	$13 \times 9 \times 2$	3.5 L	$33 \times 23 \times 5$
Loaf Pan	$8 \times 4 \times 3$	1.5 L	$20 \times 10 \times 7$
	$9 \times 5 \times 3$	2 L	$23 \times 13 \times 7$
Round Layer	$8 \times 1 1/2$	1.2 L	20×4
Cake Pan	$9 \times 1 1/2$	1.5 L	23×4
Pie Plate	$8 \times 1 1/4$	750 mL	20×3
	$9 \times 1 1/4$	1 L	23×3
Baking Dish	1 quart	1 L	—
or Casserole	$1 1/2$ quart	1.5 L	—
	2 quart	2 L	—